It
    was
        you
    all
        along

Also by RUSS

IT'S ALL IN YOUR HEAD

what if you're the one
you've been waiting for?

It

was

you

all

along

RUSS

HARPER

An Imprint of HarperCollins*Publishers*

IT WAS YOU ALL ALONG

Printed in Canada. No part of this book may be used or reproduced in any manner
whatsoever without written permission except in the case of brief quotations embodied
in critical articles and reviews. For information, address HarperCollins Publishers,
195 Broadway, New York, NY 10007.

HarperCollins books may be purchased for educational, business, or sales promotional
use. For information, please email the Special Markets Department at
SPsales@harpercollins.com.

FIRST EDITION
Designed by Adham Foda

Library of Congress Cataloging-in-Publication Data has been applied for.

ISBN 978-0-06-335788-4

24 25 26 27 28 TC   10 9 8 7 6 5 4 3 2 1

I dedicate this book to you.

CONTENTS

INTRO

In 2019, I thought I'd pulled myself back from the brink. I had let the chaos of my life drag me to a dark place. The journey up until that point had always been me versus me, but somewhere along the way it had morphed into me versus the world. I took a break from social media and decided not to tour. I put all my feelings into my music and I wrote my first book.

When I wrote IT'S ALL IN YOUR HEAD I thought I was handing you the cheat codes to success. I was sure I had all the answers. I put everything I knew about pursuing your dream in that book and thought I'd never have to write anything ever again. But the last chapter of IT'S ALL IN YOUR HEAD could have been the first chapter of this book.

Back then, I did know that sometimes you have to step back and remember that you can't control the world, but what you can control are your thoughts and how you show up in the world. I did know that success is not a final destination. I did know that when you are down and you rise up, you feel more powerful than you ever did. But I didn't know that I was at the very beginning of a journey of self-mastery. Over the last four years I've learned enough to know how much shit I don't know. So, I won't pretend this book holds everything. But it does hold everything I know so far.

Don't beat up your younger self for not knowing what you know now. You can only use the tools you've acquired up until that point. The mindset is to keep your toolbox open.

Make sure you're taking the time to self-reflect and take inventory of what is going on internally. Don't be so rigid that you fail to recognize when it is time to course correct.

Success is in the journey.

When we were seventeen, my best friend, Bugus, and I educated ourselves with a small stash of books about success. Those books helped define the path I was on. But there was another book I read back then about a different kind of success that lodged itself deep in my brain, Paulo Coelho's *The Alchemist*. In it, Santiago leaves his homeland of Andalusia to chase a treasure he believes he will find at the pyramids in Egypt. I can't tell you what the treasure is or whether Santiago finds it. What I can tell you is what Paulo Coelho told me: One man's story is every man's story. We are all lost trying to find our treasure.

Something made me pick up *The Alchemist* again during the summer of 2021. That book got me through a tough season. As I read, I started making a new album, *Santiago*. I made beats, came up with hooks, worked with collaborators, but I couldn't finish the project. Something was holding me back. Subconsciously, I was hung up on one question: What's my treasure? What am I going after truly? At first, I thought the treasure was going number one, but that didn't resonate. It didn't feel real. I didn't finish the album.

I had achieved so many measures of success but I didn't know what was next in my career or my life. I was just putting out songs and going through the motions. I wasn't sure what my destination was anymore. I had forgotten that success is not a final destination. The album felt aimless. So did I.

Having definite aim, no matter what area of your life it is in, is so important. Everyone needs a mountain to climb.

By the end of that year, I felt heavy—spiritually,

mentally, physically. I didn't know where I was trying to go in my career. I didn't know where I was trying to go in my personal life or in my spiritual life. I was overwhelmed. I felt like I had no purpose. I didn't know where to go or what to do. Lying in my bed one night, I started to spiral. I freaked out and broke down crying.

Up to this point I had thought that the secret to feeling good about myself lay in my next achievement—that if I could just get a number one song then I'd feel good about myself. If I could just get that girl, then I'd feel good. If I can just get my mom that beach house, I would feel good. Then I started doing all that stuff and it didn't work. I didn't feel good. I still felt this hole. That's the journey I'm on right now: I'm trying to fill my own hole.

In the days after my breakdown, I talked to Bugus and I turned to books. Books change lives. I read self-help books, I started working on self-discipline, and I kept thinking about *The Alchemist*, which had set me on a path. As I've traveled along, I've written down what I'm learning. Books have helped me along my journey, and I hope this book will help you along on yours.

This journey is not just about your career; it is not just about your romantic relationships. It is not about achieving the external markers of success—going platinum or earning a million dollars. All of that means nothing if you are still losing to yourself. Your external world will reflect the state of your internal world. All aspects of your life warrant being checked in on and improved. Pursue your best self. Your best self is your whole self. Mastering your self is a game that you can play for the rest of your life. You are on a quest of self-mastery and self-love. Success is a never-ending inside job.

Your best self is your whole self.

01

PERFECTIONIST

PERFECTION IS AN ILLUSION

So many of us make the dangerous assumption that we're supposed to be perfect. Perfection isn't real. It's an illusion that keeps us in a place of fear and shame.

My dad's metric for success was perfection—whether it was doing the dishes or making sure the forks faced the right way in the dishwasher; the car had to be packed a certain way and in a certain time frame, and when and if things weren't done just as he wanted, he would snap and belittle all of us. Everything had to be his way, the perfect way. It was his world, and it was a pressure cooker. When I was a kid my dad coached my basketball teams, and during games he was very critical. I was eight. If someone flew by me when I was playing defense he'd scream *OLÉ!* at me as if I was a matador that had just let the bull past, which made me feel dumb and embarrassed. School was easy for me, but bringing home grades was intense. I would bring home an A−, and my father would say, "Imagine if you studied." Or, "Imagine if you applied yourself." Even the A's weren't good enough. (My dad would say in response to that, "Well it wasn't an A, it was an A−.") It doesn't seem that heavy, but after years of it, I began to feel like nothing I did was ever good enough.

As I got older, his impossible standards drove a wedge between us.

When you do anything creative, especially at the beginning, your confidence can be fragile because you're new and unsure, and you want approval. Sometimes the wrong no from the right person can be really damaging.

When I started making music I'd show my dad a video I'd shot or play him a song. He wouldn't acknowledge the effort; he'd delve into critiques. "Why did you shoot it this way?" or "You should write lyrics like this." Then he'd go in for the kill,

"You'd be so much further ahead in your career if you'd just listen to me." Just once, I wanted him to say, "That's awesome. I'm proud of you for going after what you love. Keep going."

When I was twenty, we had a big blowup after I'd done my first interview. I was so excited to show it to him. When you're going after something that is so far away—like, another-planet-far-away—any sign of progress makes you feel like you could arrive tomorrow. Instead of recognizing the progress I'd made, he just started criticizing the interview. Granted, I was very drunk and the interview was very sloppy, but I wanted him to be excited that on this planet that I told him I was going to travel to, there were signs of life.

"You wonder why none of us kids don't bring anything to you, why we don't talk to you about anything," I exploded. "You just shit on everything."

We started getting in each other's faces and

my brother, Frank, had to break it up. I stayed with Frank for a couple of days, then I went to LA for a month and got a tattoo of a rosary made of music notes on my arm. It was my way of declaring that music was my religion, but deeper than that, it was me digging my heels into the sand and saying, *This is who I am and this is what I'm doing.* It made my commitment to this wild dream feel real. It also had the added benefit of announcing to my father that I was not going to get a regular fucking job. I was going to make this dream come true.

But as hard as I pushed against him, he had wormed his way deep into my brain. My inner critic was really my dad's voice, which over time, morphed into my own. My dad was hypercritical, had unmeetable standards, and, at times, his love felt conditional. I adopted my dad's metric as my own, so that I was never good enough for myself.

I was raised in an environment where making

mistakes was met with shame instead of understanding. Perfection was the standard. Anything less wasn't good enough. This seed of shame blossomed into a false sense of omnipotence. I thought I was supposed to know the right turn at every intersection. Naturally, I made a lot of "wrong" turns, and when I did, I would first try to defend my turn to the death of me out of fear of facing the harsh reality that I was not perfect. What came after that inevitably was deep shame and humiliation. I beat myself up, embarrassed that I could be so stupid.

Why did you not know what do in this brand-new moment that you have no experience in, you fucking idiot? That's a toned-down sarcastic version of some of the self-talk that would ensue upon making any mistake. I hated being human. I hated myself, unless I was perfect. I loved myself, conditionally.

I believed that if I beat myself up enough for making a mistake, I wouldn't make any more mistakes.

My perfectionism early in my career blocked me from taking accountability of my mistakes and learning from them. One place I derailed myself with my perfectionism was in interviews.

I had been studying industry interviews since I was seventeen, and when I finally was in the chair myself, I wanted to be perfect. I wanted to make sure I said all the best things and that I came off as cool and suave, and not just overconfident and braggadocious.

The pressure for perfection was amplified because as a white guy in rap, I was, naturally, shunned from the culture and was desperately seeking its approval. As a kid, I'd felt ostracized from my dad—I wanted his approval and I didn't get it. As an adult I effectively re-created my childhood environment, replacing my dad with the rap industry. These interviews felt like a big opportunity.

But, sober me was nervous and insecure about being my authentic self in culturally valuable places. I didn't trust my sober self to be good enough. I thought that if I drank I'd be perfect. Instead, because I was drinking, I was saying shit and doing too much and spiraling out of control, and overcompensating. Those drunken interviews sparked a lot of the hate and negativity I received. Had I just been sober and sat with my insecurities I wouldn't have said half the shit I said.

The resistance of my insecurities lead to self-implosive behaviors, such as losing my cool and getting too riled up in interviews.

I've learned that resisting my insecurities leads to self-destruction.

My perfectionism hindered me from manifesting more success. Because more success meant more fame which meant even less room for error, which only amplified my need for perfection, which caused immense anxiety.

"

YOUR FEAR IS THE CONTAINER OF YOUR GREATNESS.

"

When you are afraid of success, you subconsciously command the universe to keep you stagnant. You are communicating that you're only good with this level because you can manage this level. If you let go of that fear, let go of that need for perfectionism, how much bigger could your success be?

"

YOU NEED LESS CRITICISM AND MORE COMPASSION.

"

Perfectionism is a hamster wheel powered by fear and shame, and the only way to get off it is having compassion for yourself and extending it to others. Compassion requires patience.

You made mistakes. You weren't perfect. You're a human. The intolerance of our own mistakes is an intolerance of the process of learning. It is the antithesis of being patient with ourselves and giving ourselves grace and the space to figure things out.

02

LOSIN' CONTROL

TRUST STARTS WITH LETTING GO

Early on, I branded myself as a do-it-myself guy. I preached self-sufficiency, which is a valuable skill. But there is another layer to it: I didn't trust help, so it was imperative that I controlled everything.

For me, help was always code for criticism. Perfectionists run from criticism. When people try to help me, whether it's my girl or a colleague, I take it as criticism and get defensive. When someone says, "Hey, maybe you should do . . . ," I hear, "I didn't do a good enough job." And as soon as I thought I wasn't perfect, I'd beat myself up. If I accepted criticism it would mean accepting that I'm not perfect. And if I'm not perfect . . . who am I?

Perfectionism is a lonely trap. It is rooted in shame and it is not exclusive to ourselves—we can foist that shame onto others.

It's no surprise that I had zero tolerance for other people's mistakes.

"

MICROMANAGING IS A FORM OF CONTROL THAT ROBS PEOPLE OF THEIR OWN SELF-TRUST AND POWER.

"

How we treat others is often a reflection of how we treat ourselves.

I had no patience with myself; therefore, I had no patience with anyone in my life—that goes for family, friends, and coworkers. No one was safe from the wrath of the all-knowing king (what a douchebag). If they did anything that was less than perfect, I was right there to degrade and belittle them.

The part I failed to realize was that shaming someone every time they make a mistake doesn't lead to competence. It leads to bitterness and resentment. Trying to control every aspect of everything ends up robbing your coworkers, collaborators, and family of their power. It kills their confidence and robs them of their individuality/ sovereignty/autonomy until they don't know whether to shit or wind their watch. The once-concrete foundation of who they are has been replaced with eggshells. We need to heal so that the blood from our self-inflicted wounds doesn't drip onto someone who didn't cut us.

I wanted help but didn't know how to let myself be helped. Things had to be done my way (perfect), and I trusted only myself to uphold that standard. I needed to loosen up my control in order to allow room for someone to come in and give me the help that I actually wanted.

I probably talk to my manager more than anyone else. We're often on the phone because something in my career is pissing me off. He is the liaison and the buffer. So, he catches a lot of shit. Countless times I have heavily criticized how he does what he does. "Why did you do this?" "Why didn't you say that?" Starting off almost any sentence with "why" is shame-based. The subtext is: How could you be so stupid?

That's the way I spoke to myself. That's the way my dad spoke to me.

Those harsh, shame-based reactions come from a deep desire to control a situation. Often we want to control a situation because we lack trust. If you don't trust someone emotionally to take care of you, you will try to control them. You shame people for their mistakes, because you don't trust them to do the right thing. When we have to protect ourselves fiercely, we have a hard time trusting people.

But when you pounce on someone, saying things like, "This is how you fucked up," and demanding to know "Why did you do this?," you're not trusting them to take accountability and course-correct. And you are creating a space where trust cannot grow.

When something goes wrong, instead of pouncing, ask the person what happened, or what's going on with them. Give them space to feel safe enough to say what's going on, because that fosters trust and depth in the relationship. Of course, it takes time to relinquish perfectionism and control. It also requires a lot of practice.

Step one is awareness. If you are aware, you can catch yourself. Step two is self-regulation. When I feel myself spiraling up and that language starts to flare in my brain, I try to catch it before it comes out.

When I shamed my manager he would get defensive, and we would end up talking in circles. Now when I call my manager, I try not to criticize or shame him. I try to honestly express what's really bothering *me*.

Imagine seeing a scary-looking dog that's barking crazily and grinning and showing you its teeth. All it's trying to do is tell you it wants you to pet him, but you're probably not going to be receptive to that dog language—as opposed to that same dog lying down, rolling over, showing you its stomach, and inviting you to pet it.

Barking was how we communicated in the environment I grew up in. But when there are real emotions and a real experience that I'm trying to get my manager—or anyone I talk to—to understand, they're not going to be able to receive what I'm trying to tell them if I'm barking at them.

Instead of demanding to know why something went the way it did, I ask him to tell me what happened. He has more sovereignty and also more accountability. He's also a lot quicker to say, "My bad," because I'm not putting him on the defense. The communication barriers are dropped.

When, instead of reprimanding people, you open communication and allow them room to own their actions, they have more bandwidth, spiritually and mentally, to do what needs to be done.

"

WHEN YOU GIVE PEOPLE THE PERMISSION TO BE WRONG WITHOUT THE PROMISE OF PUNISHMENT, YOU ALLOW SPACE FOR TRUST, ACCOUNTABILITY, AND COMMUNICATION TO GROW.

"

03

PAID OFF

DISCIPLINE IS AN ACT OF LOVE, NOT PUNISHMENT

It was January 2022.

I was thirty pounds overweight. The tequila and lack of portion control had finally caught up to me. I had no discipline over my eating habits, let alone my thoughts, desires, or emotions. I was losing to myself.

Discipline was the lifeboat that saved me from the sinking I was suffering.

In the days after, I read *Outwitting the Devil* by Napoleon Hill. The book had been sitting on my shelf for years. Bugus's brother had given it to me and I'd never read it. Hill writes about mastering your three appetites: your actual nourishment appetite—what you're putting in your body; your sexual appetite; and the appetite to express loosely formed opinions, which by now, I'm sure you are well aware, is a particular weakness of mine.

Discipline sometimes has negative connotations. For a lot of us, the word "discipline" evokes doing shit you don't want to do but have to. It is associated with being militaristic and harsh, and often thought of as a punishment.

The reality is, I don't necessarily WANT to get up early and work out.

I don't want to say no to that pizza.

I don't want to "settle down."

But I HAVE to if I want to be the person that I strive to be.

Doing things in your control that are hard is going to feel uncomfortable. But it's an act of self-love that better prepares you for the hard shit that's out of your control.

"

**MAKING DECISIONS THAT ALIGN
WITH THE IDENTITY OF THE
PERSON YOU WANT TO BE IS A
CELEBRATION, NOT A PUNISHMENT.**

"

There are a lot of things that aren't in our control in life. What you put in your body isn't one of them.

In 2020, when I was at my peak of disgusting behavior—eating like crap, drinking too much, and not having a normal sleep regimen—my brother, Frank, and his girlfriend, a personal trainer, lived with me for a few months. Frank is in crazy shape. He does jujitsu and works out every day and makes his living as a nutritionist. Fitness is his way of being. The two of them would buzz around the house—exercising and cooking this crazy good food, and introducing me to these healthy alternatives.

I wish I could tell you I was immediately inspired to get healthy. I wasn't, but after hitting that low point, I turned to my brother.

When you know someone whose body looks healthy and you see how they actually live, you get a lot of clarity about the changes you need to make. I was a fucking slob. I didn't change right away but I did begin to think that maybe I should get it together.

By the top of 2022, I was fed up with how I felt, so I locked in with Frank. He instructed me on how much to eat and I stuck to it, cooking all my meals and tracking everything I ate, and we started working out together. It was a really beautiful thing to have that point of connection with him and to be doing something positive. Working on your body and your health with someone that close to you is awesome.

After about eight months I had lost thirty pounds of fat. But something more impactful happened—my discipline multiplied and showed up in other areas of my life.

Just like negative habits multiply, so do positive ones. When you discipline one aspect of your life, disciplining another becomes easier.

Discipling your sexual appetite is imperative, especially for young men. Sexual appetite is often misdirected energy.

Most of the time, I have a lot of energy running through my body. It's excited, anxious, and jolts from head to toe leaving me feeling charged, like I want to run full speed around a track for seventy-eight hours, or have sex. Having all that energy all the time can feel like a superpower. But how will you use that power? Throughout my twenties, unbeknownst to me, I was always looking for somewhere to put this energy. As my access to women increased, sex became the easiest and, at the time, most fulfilling bank to deposit that energy into. Many young men have that feeling, and the only place they know they can put that energy is in sex—which can be getting sucked into porn or being promiscuous. Sometimes it's not that you necessarily have a crazy sex drive; it's more about having all this excited energy with no outlet for it.

When I was a kid I played basketball all the time. I played on a team that practiced before and after school, and then I'd come home from school, throw down my backpack, and run out down to the neighborhood park and play more basketball and tackle football with my friends. I ran out all my energy on that big field, and by the time I got home, that energy had settled to a manageable cruising altitude. As a kid I wasn't aware that I had this energy, because it always had something or someone to keep it entertained and engaged. As I got older and started living a more sedentary lifestyle, I started noticing the energy. I'd wake up and sit in my house with that same youthful enthusiastic excited energy. The difference is that it had nowhere to go. Well, it had two places—the studio and the bedroom. And if I didn't feel like going to the studio I would call a woman over. I used sex to expend my energy, self-soothe, and ultimately regulate my nervous system.

Sexual energy is beautiful when exchanged with someone you love and care about deeply. When it's frivolous, though, it can be self-destructive.

I had read at a young age that highly successful men are highly sexed people, so I walked around proud of this sexual energy. The problem with this line of thinking is that when you only think the energy is sexual, you're gonna think that sex is the only place for it to go. If you can reframe how you look at it and recognize it as JUST energy, you open yourself up to exploring the possibilities of other outlets for that energy.

The first step in disciplining your sexual energy is reclassifying it as *just energy*. After awareness comes action. Let me understand what's happening. Let me take inventory: Okay, I have all this excited energy. Do I want to go to the gym? Do I want to go for a run? Do I want to practice my craft? Do I want to just sit with it and breathe through it and work on self-regulating? Or do I want to call up a random woman, then sit on the couch afterward and wait for the nervous energy to pop back up again?

Who do I want to be? What choice can I make that will authentically align with my identity?

Disciplining my thoughts (I'm a classic overthinker) seemed like an impossible task, and for a while it was. But that's because nothing else in my life was disciplined. Once I disciplined my eating habits and my energy, my mind was better conditioned to be disciplined, and I noticed a change mentally. I had a more stable existence. There are still bumps and dips, but as my discipline grows, the highs and lows aren't as extreme.

To discipline my thoughts, I wanted to control my impulses to express loosely formed opinions and also control my overthinking—which were things that got me into trouble with others and with myself.

One loosely formed opinion that got me into hot water was when I wore a T-shirt that read: HOW MUCH XANS AND LEAN DO YOU HAVE TO DO BEFORE YOU REALIZE YOU'RE A FUCKING LOSER. That was a loosely formed, ill-phrased opinion that went viral and, understandably, got a lot of negative pushback because of my perceived insensitivity toward people suffering from addiction. What I really wanted to do was to raise awareness, to discourage people from trying dangerous drugs, and to encourage them to interrogate their motivation for wanting to try them in the first place.

I was once a kid who was curious about lean, because I heard about it in a rap song. That was lame. Thankfully I had somebody older in my life telling me how dumb that was. I stand by my motivation, but the T-shirt was an extremely loosely formed opinion, and for a message that is that serious, I should have spent more time crafting and articulating what I was really trying to say.

Imagine your mind is a fortress guarded by an army. When you don't have discipline in your life, the soldiers are on their phones, dozing, goofing off, playing cards, bullshitting. ANYTHING can get by them. My own negative thoughts were my enemy, and they were slipping by my army all day every day. It's not the soldiers' fault. They had no training. However, when you start introducing discipline, those soldiers go through boot camp until they evolve into an elite group of soldiers, like the King's Guard. Everyone is standing at attention and is laser-focused on securing and protecting the fortress.

Discipline is the epitome of self-love and self-respect. Respect your body. Respect your mind. Respect your energy. Honor the gift of your health, life, and freedom. When you treat yourself with discipline, you're treating yourself with love.

04

ENOUGH

EXCESS WILL NEVER EQUAL ENOUGH

When my parents got divorced, unbeknownst to me, I was thrust into the role of head of the family. Instead of going to my father, my mom would come to me for things. It gave me a newfound respect for what my dad did for our family—financially. When I stepped into the role of head of household, my mom started coming to me for more emotional support, and I felt the emotional responsibility of everyone coming to me. As I gained success, I provided for my family—emotionally and financially. Since I was a kid my identity has been wrapped up in saving everyone else. When you're a kid, if you feel like your mom isn't safe from herself, it feels like life or death. In my childhood, I played the role of emotional savior with my mom a lot. When her and my dad would fight, she would storm off and lock herself in the bathroom and cry. I was the only one in the family who would go to her and make sure she was okay. I was really worried about her from a very early age. I had to be enough for her and my family because the stakes were so high. I believed that if I made a misstep, if I wasn't enough, my family wouldn't be safe. That continued into adulthood and was compounded by the financial responsibility I took on.

As an adult, that fear of not being enough invaded everything. On a visceral level, I believed that if I didn't get industry approval, then I was in danger. When I didn't hit certain marks, I actually had a physical trauma response. That was my body telling me: You're in danger. My whole life there has always been an undercurrent of frantic, desperate energy—sadness, fear, and anxiety.

For a lot of men, and for a lot of people in rap, it's pretty standard to build a fortress around your emotions, so that you never appear vulnerable. I was never able to face my deepest emotions. Growing up, I was taught to brush it off and keep going, so that's what I did for a long, long time.

The only place I found relief was in music. Music is your soul trying to communicate. So I would sit in the studio every day for hours because it distracted me from my anxiety. I used to say that music was my therapist, but it wasn't. I expressed my anxiety, my emotions, and my fear in my music, but they were still inside me, undealt with.

I was never enough for my mom or my dad, and so I was never enough for myself. My dad was hypercritical with an impossible standard of perfection, and my mom was never content for longer than two minutes. I was doomed from the start.

DISCLAIMER: I don't blame my parents for anything. I love them and accept them for who they are. They've done a great job. Blaming them would perpetuate the shame cycle. The reality is, everyone, including our parents, are human (shocker). And humans all have childhood trauma issues that manifest into adult hurdles.

But we all have childhood experiences that have ripple effects in our adulthood, that we have to become aware of and learn how to contend with—and possibly unlearn behaviors that aren't serving us. It's our job to figure out who we are and to figure out why we are. And then it's our job to figure out who we want to be. Once you understand why you do certain things, then you can decide what you are going to do about those behaviors. What you do will be guided by who you want to be.

Not feeling good enough has been the main component of my fierce ambition. A lot of people credit my success to my ambition. But, at some point, never feeling good enough, no matter your ambition, isn't sustainable. From the outside looking in, people would say, "Wow you're so driven, that's so admirable." If you only knew who was driving and where we were going.

My insecurities were behind the wheel and we were driving full speed toward external recognition. We thought that would make us feel good enough, but when perfection is the standard, there is no destination. You're on a NASCAR track doing perpetual loops chasing yourself.

Going platinum wasn't good enough.

My inner critic taunted me:

"Why didn't you go platinum sooner?

You only went 1x platinum?

That's not good enough."

Buying my mom a beach house wasn't good enough.

"Why isn't her house on the actual sand with a balcony that faces the water that can also see the sunset on the water year round?"

Making a million dollars wasn't good enough.

"Make another million. One isn't enough.

You'll have enough after two."

Sleeping with a model wasn't good enough.

"You didn't sleep with that one though.

 After her, you'll feel good enough then."

You get the point. None of these things ever made me feel good enough, because the gift of external validation was an empty box in attractive wrapping.

You can shame yourself into victory but you will feel like you lost.

Growing up in a pressure cooker can create highly successful people. Lots of inordinately successful people have a kind of fucked-up drive that gets them to a place of overwhelming success.

But it's not sustainable. Being in a heavily criticized environment—whether that's your home, your office, or your head—where shame is your greatest motivation, is damaging.

DRINKIN' TO FORGET THAT BEIN' YOU IS NOT ENOUGH

— "I LOVE YOU BOY"

Many of us assume the grass is greener in front of the bigger house. Sometimes it is. The fallacy is thinking that the grass being greener means more than what's going on inside the home. I have everything that you could think would be the fix-all for a person not feeling good about themselves—the money, the mansion, the glamor, the external validation, the greener grass—which is why I'm able to say that's not what's going to do it. That way of thinking is what led me to my breakdown.

I chased after all these external things that didn't make me feel better about myself, and I still felt empty.

You can have "everything" and feel nothing.

Excess will never equal enough. Feeling enough is a gift I have to give to myself—and it starts with self-recognition.

"

**KNOWING YOU ARE
ENOUGH BEGINS WITH AN
ACKNOWLEDGMENT OF WHERE
YOU ARE, A CELEBRATION OF WHAT
YOU'VE DONE, AND GRACE FOR
WHAT YOU HAVEN'T DONE.**

"

To feel enough you must take inventory. Learn to recognize what doesn't fill the hole no matter how much of it you have. Become aware of what's going on internally so that you can accurately assess what you're lacking and what you need.

A lot of my ambition was me chasing a feeling. I was perpetually chasing this idea that if I do *that*, I could feel good about myself. If I accomplish *that*, I can feel good about myself. What I didn't know was that really what I was chasing was myself.

CHAPTER

05

LAST NIGHT

GRIEVE THE ENDING OF
EACH CHAPTER

I DIDNT KNOW THAT LAST NIGHT WAS OUR LAST NIGHT TOGETHER, DID YOU?

— "LAST NIGHT"

My mom surprised us with a little shih tzu puppy when I was in high school. I named her Allegra, and from the beginning she was my dog. Her name meant "happy" in Italian. She slept in my room and if I shut the door, she'd scratch at it until I let her in. When there was thunder, she'd find me and press her trembling, furry white body against my belly. We moved around a lot in Georgia, and she was with us in every single house, and part of most of my childhood memories. For fourteen years she carried me through life.

Her death was a line of demarcation.

Getting a therapist had been on my to-do list for years—I even talked about needing therapy in my songs. But when Allegra died in July 2022, an unbearable weight pressed down on me. I didn't know exactly what it was, but I knew that I needed somebody to talk to.

I had my first therapy session right before the European tour that was slated to start in August. We met on Zoom. Connor was a young guy, about to turn forty, with a very calm, nonjudgmental energy.

I was excited to talk to him. For the longest time, I didn't have anywhere to go with my shit, and I would start feeling crazy and irritable, because I had so much pent-up pain and anger and frustration and chaos and nowhere to put it. Sometimes I didn't feel like going to the studio. I'd let it fester, and it would come out in self-destructive habits—drinking or promiscuity or overeating. Having a therapist means I have a place to go to for help.

A mixture of arrogance and fear had stopped me from getting a therapist sooner.

Part of me felt like I could figure everything out on my own. Part of me was embarrassed. I didn't know how to even approach the conversation. I didn't know who to call. And part of me kept telling myself, *You're a bitch if you do that.* The idea of getting a therapist, as attractive as it sounded, also directly threatened my idea of what a man was. When I told that to Connor, he said, "Society measures a man based on how much they can carry, how far they can carry it, and how long they can carry it."

During the first session I talked to him about grieving the end of my childhood and grieving the end of chapters in your life. He helped me to understand why Allegra's death had opened up this well of grief in me.

"You've been going through really big changes in your life. Have you ever taken time to grieve the transition from being anonymous to being famous, grieve no longer feeling like a son or a brother now that you are taking responsibility and care of the whole family? Did you ever grieve?"

I hadn't. Everything had just kind of happened. I'd found myself playing this role and feeling like I was never enough.

Boom, we started peeling back the layers. He was like Morpheus in *The Matrix*—he came into the game and unplugged me from all the bullshit I was subscribing to. Sometimes I wish I could go back to sleep. But I can't. I'm on a new path, aware and learning to move forward—awake.

After Allegra died and I started therapy, I woke up to the idea that I had to grieve my childhood. I needed to grieve the role I used to play in the family. I had friendships that had ended. I had left behind being a regular guy with anonymity. Essentially, I had to grieve all the old versions of me. I haven't had a lot of moments in my life where it's been very clear that one chapter is ending and another is beginning. For a lot of people those markers come with the beginning and end of things like college or jobs or the moment you bought your first home. I didn't go to college, I didn't have a "job," and my twenties were a storm of so many wild things happening one after another that I lost sight of beginnings and endings. It was all a blur.

Finally, I began to recognize all the chapters that had ended. So many pages had turned, and I could've sworn I had just picked up the book.

Ritualizing the beginnings and the endings of chapters is so important. If you don't define each period in your life, you don't know when things started or ended, and it's all just one big fucking blur of life.

Recognizing each chapter helps us reevaluate our goals at every step of the journey. This reevaluation also helps you evolve your goals. If your goal is vague—like, I want to be successful— then you won't know when you've arrived. But when you break down your success into small parts, you can enjoy each cresting wave, and utilize each floating period.

Sometimes you're driving around your old neighborhood, or you hear an old song, and you're hit with a wave of nostalgia. You remember an old life. You remember being a kid. Then you realize how much time has passed and that you never went to the funeral of your own childhood. Or you never went to the funeral of that phase of your life.

We experience so much grief that we don't acknowledge. The end of a family. A friendship. A project. How many times have you lost someone or something and thought, *I never even said goodbye?*

We need to normalize throwing funerals for chapters in our life. There are numerous ways to grieve and to celebrate. You can do it internally. You can do it publicly, or you can do it with a small community. Theaters have opening-night parties and closing-night toasts; we have celebrations when babies are born and wakes when people die. The chapters of your life come and go with blessings and obstacles, and we have to acknowledge them so that we can honor them, celebrate them, say goodbye, and accept that it's time for a new chapter.

Right after that session and right before I left for the European tour, I had an argument with my mom that conjured up all these emotions. Therapy had opened the floodgates of feelings that I had pushed down for years. I was hit by a tidal wave.

I was overwhelmed by everything that had been going on in my life over the past several years. I didn't feel like a son anymore. I didn't feel like a brother anymore. Because I was the head of the family. That sat heavy on me. When I argued with my mom, all the pressures, anxieties, and extreme changes over the past years that I never took the time to grieve for bubbled to the surface. And then, I left for tour.

I arrived in the first city, Stuttgart, Germany. The day of the first show I was so down, my spirit was checked out. Before a show I always run through a little bit of my performance to get my body ready. I was in the hotel room trying to get ready to perform. I couldn't even lift my arm to go through the motions as if I was onstage. I looked at my reflection. I can't do this. This was day one of twenty-eight cities. The whirlpool of my emotions was going to pull me under unless I pulled myself out.

I looked at myself in the mirror. I knew I would be nothing onstage. I wasn't going to make it.

Doubt slipped around my brain. What are my fans going to do if I cancel the tour? What is my mom going to do? She's going to feel like it's her fault. What's my brother going to feel? I always took everyone else's feelings into consideration, everyone's except my own.

I've always prided myself on being perfect, being strong, keeping it all together, and being positive. Canceling a tour and letting people down wasn't in my makeup. I needed everyone to like me. I need everyone to approve of me. I needed to be enough for everyone else.

But I couldn't do it. I felt defeated. This was the worst moment of my life.

I didn't go on.

I canceled that day of the show.

I didn't want to go on because I knew I wasn't

going to be able to give a performance up to my standards. That was compounded by the anxiety I had about dealing with the potential criticism of a lackluster show. But my not going on was also letting all these people down—my fans, my manager, the promoter, my family. But the real question was whether I was letting myself down if I canceled, or was I letting myself down if I didn't.

I wrangled with that question. I was on the phone bouncing back and forth between Connor and Bugus talking everything through. When I decided to cancel that night's show and the tour they were both really understanding.

It was hard for me to tell myself that I was canceling, but by the time I called my manager, I knew what I needed, and I felt a bit of relief when I finally said it out loud in an official capacity. For a moment, I felt lighter.

My manager didn't argue. Just like Connor and

Bugus, he was really supportive; he always is. He told me briefly what it would mean contractually and then told me not to worry about anything. He would take care of it.

Everyone in my family was so confused. Frank was with me on tour, and a few minutes later he texted me: I'M OUTSIDE YOUR DOOR.

I have been in hundreds and hundreds of hotels around the world, and this is the only hotel that had a camera by the door that showed what's outside the room.

On the tiny screen I saw my brother sitting outside my door. I didn't open the door. I didn't talk to him.

I texted him: WHY ARE YOU AT MY DOOR?

Frank: BECAUSE I'M YOUR BROTHER.

Me: I DON'T FEEL LIKE TALKING.

Still, he sat outside my room for hours in case I needed him.

That afternoon I wrote a post telling my fans. It was one of the hardest things for me to do, and it was also one of the most important things I've ever done:

I have to cancel the European tour. I could make up excuses so that I don't lose money but the reality is mentally I feel like shit. In the last 24 hours shit happened that has led to some extremely lonely and empty realizations about things in my family life that have my head feeling like it's gonna burst. I feel terrible about doing this to my European fans. If you no longer support me after this, I get it. If you don't believe my reason, I get it. I've never had to do this and I feel very defeated but I can't crash and burn and give y'all shitty performances on the way out. You will be refunded from your point of purchase. I'm very sorry and like I said, the last thing I wanna do is let my fans down which obviously, that's what I'm doing so any negative feelings any of you end up having towards me, I understand. If this happened during the middle or end of tour I'd probably push through but it happening before the first show, knowing that I gotta go out and give my 100% energy to 24 shows is something I cannot do. I truly don't expect people to care or to have empathy. Everyone has their own shit they gotta deal with. I just ask y'all to try to understand that maybe you *don't* understand…that in it of itself *is* understanding. I need time to make sense of certain things and for once I need to put myself first. I'm really sorry. I love y'all.

We didn't fly home until the next day. My mom had left early, so it was just me and my brother and my girl and my manager. I didn't want to talk to anyone. I didn't want to be around anyone at the airport or on the plane. I didn't know how I was supposed to act. I didn't feel comfortable. I just wanted to get the fuck out of there to get the fuck away from everyone.

The flight home was brutal. Landing in Atlanta was brutal—once I was back the reality of the situation hit me. I had built a beautiful golden palace fit for a king, but inside was rubble.

Stepping off the plane, riding in the car, walking through my front door, I knew I was returning to the rubble without having done the thing I said I was going to do. I felt like a failure. I felt like I'd lost to myself. You versus You: as if somehow the vulnerable and hurting version of me had taken down the successful, unbreakable me.

For the longest time I felt like a high achiever. I went after things. I took on challenges. I had conquered the world. But I hadn't conquered my own trauma and issues. There is a whole world inside me that I had neglected. I thought I hadn't given up on anything in my entire life. But that wasn't true. I'd given up on taking care of myself. The truth was, when I canceled my tour, I was putting my well-being first for the first time in my life.

Immediately, I felt like shit, and the blowback was ruthless. I had always gotten my self-worth from not letting people down, from always being there for people, from being perfect, not showing any weakness. Showing weakness publicly and letting people down publicly was excruciating.

Fans destroyed me. I had expected that. There I was, Mr. Manifest, law-of-attraction believer, self-help book author, in pain and vulnerable very publicly. But some fans also supported me. In hard moments you see who really supports you and who believes in you. I tried not to get caught up in what people were saying. The biggest question, of course, was how I would show up for myself.

In that moment, all I knew was that I needed space to grieve. There was so much shit that I had to say goodbye to.

Even though canceling the tour seemed like a step backward, it was actually a huge leap forward. It was the first time in my life that I had not resisted the pain I felt. I sat in it and I took care of myself. That was growth. No doubt, it took time for me to see that.

"

THE ENDING OF EACH CHAPTER OF YOUR LIFE NEEDS ITS OWN COMMEMORATION OR YOU WILL BE OVERWHELMED BY THE TIDAL WAVE OF CHANGE AT AN INOPPORTUNE TIME.

"

06

THAT WAS ME

BE A DIEHARD FAN OF YOURSELF

My first show after canceling the tour was at the pyramids in Egypt.

In 2020 I had been invited to perform at the pyramids on my birthday to a crowd of ten thousand people. I felt like Santiago, on the cusp of finding my treasure. The pyramids!

But, then, the event was rescheduled because of the pandemic, and when I actually did the show two years later, it wasn't on my birthday. It was in October, a few months and many therapy sessions after I'd canceled the tour.

Still, it was the pyramids, and I was the first solo rapper to perform there—EVER. I can't lie—there was a small part of me that felt that this was going to be the thing that pushed me over the top. People would have to respect me once they'd seen me performing at the pyramids.

When the tickets went on sale, a barrage of fans started hitting me up, telling me the tickets were too expensive and they couldn't afford them. "Please can you lower the ticket prices?" The world looked very different in the fall of 2022, and Egypt was struggling economically. We went to the promoter and told them they needed to lower the ticket prices. The promoter explained that if we lowered the ticket prices that lots of different people would be able to afford the tickets, but there'd be a greater risk of crime.

"If we lower the ticket prices, that means that we're not going to make as much money, which means you can't make the money that you were supposed to make," the promoter said. "And if we lower the ticket prices, we have to increase security, because it's going to be sketchy. But increasing security costs more money, money that we wouldn't have if you lowered the ticket prices." It was a catch-22.

Eventually, they did come down on the prices, a little. But as the ticket count updates came in, I felt lousy. My perfectionism was flaring—I wasn't going to sell ten thousand tickets. There were two sources of disappointment: I didn't want to disappoint my fans and I didn't want to disappoint myself.

The honest truth is when I get fixated on how something is supposed to be, it's very hard for me to come off of that. For two years, I thought I would be performing at the pyramids for ten thousand people on my birthday. I couldn't control the date of the performance, but I was fixated on the number of people.

The night of the show was beautiful: the sky was inky black, the air was cool, there was a wild stretch of sand and dark and then the pyramids, immense and ancient, lit in a rainbow of color. Stepping on that stage was surreal.

Seven songs in, my voice went out, which

happens sometimes. But I beat myself up about it. I never know what show it's going to happen in or how many songs it will take for my voice to come back. I act like everything is okay. I push harder and I let the crowd sing for me. There were *only* five thousand people there, but they carried me through.

Onstage at the heart of civilization, performing my music, I felt connected to the world by a powerful force. But when I got offstage I asked my photographer to send me some photos with the pyramids in the background.

"I couldn't get any because of the lighting," she explained.

"What are you talking about? That's the whole thing." I was pissed.

How would anyone know what I had done if there were no pictures?

Backstage after the show, all my friends were on ten. My friend Foda, who is Egyptian, was there with his father and brothers, and they were congratulating me and saying how crazy it was. Everyone around me was riding high. But I didn't feel like I had just performed at the pyramids.

My friends were trying to tell me what it was and all I could think about was what it wasn't.

A thorn of disappointment pricked at me. I couldn't stop thinking, *Man, this was only five thousand people. Why couldn't you sell ten thousand tickets at that crazy ticket price? You should have been able to.* I was worried that this show—which should have been epic—wasn't going to look big enough that people would cheer for me, and I needed their cheers to feel good about myself.

It bothered me that my photographer didn't get pictures of the pyramids, because I was banking on external recognition—I'd wanted ten thousand people, a perfect voice, and visual proof of what I had done in order to get applause from the world.

Being stuck on what I thought the show should have been kept me from celebrating.

I had performed at the pyramids, but I couldn't see the moment for what it was.

In therapy I started to see myself more clearly. At the beginning I was filled with pure shame. But gradually with each session I reclaimed myself. Like those sculptures chiseled out of massive pieces of stone: The artist chips away until the shape of the thing emerges. Therapy feels like it is chiseling away at all the bullshit that was on me. After every session I can see myself more clearly.

"

Chasing external recognition in hopes that it will lead to internal recognition is like chasing sex hoping that it leads to love.

"

Part of seeing yourself is acknowledging what you have done.

At the beginning of one session Connor asked me, "What's been going on?"

"Man, I get plaques and I get money and I just don't feel good about myself."

Then he taught me something that shifted my whole way of thinking about success:

EXTERNAL RECOGNITION – INTERNAL RECOGNITION = IMPOSTER SYNDROME

The applause I wanted from the outside was really just a reflection of the lack of applause from the inside. I was running around trying to get as many trophies as I could—whether that was women, money, sold-out shows, cars, houses, or awards—in hopes that I would finally be applauded. A lot of the time I did get applauded for those symbols of success; however, I couldn't hear the applause let alone feel it. It was drowned out by how loudly I was booing myself. Even if I could have heard others clapping, it wouldn't have mattered. The applause I was looking for was my own.

I didn't recognize my own accomplishments because I was too busy trying to get the world to recognize them. Chasing external recognition in hopes that it will lead to internal recognition is like chasing sex hoping that it leads to love. Been there, done that. It never works. You just feel emptier than before.

So many people—men and women—suffer from imposter syndrome.

You might be in a moment of triumph, sitting at the head of the table, standing onstage, receiving all this external recognition, but there still won't be any internal recognition. In moments like that you question yourself: *What am I doing here? Am I good enough to be here? What makes me deserving of this spot?* When you get everyone clapping for you, but inside, it's crickets—that's when the imposter syndrome starts kicking in. *Why are y'all clapping for me?*

Refusing to recognize yourself keeps you in a place of shame. Never being good enough for yourself locks you in a negative headspace and prevents you from having gratitude for what you've done and accomplished.

One of the first assignments my therapist gave

me was to practice self-praise. "Acknowledge something you've done that you're proud of, and list why it's important to you and how it makes you feel," he said toward the end of a session. This can feel weird and awkward, but it's invaluable. Try it.

Celebration starts with compassion and awareness. In order to celebrate yourself, you have to be aware of what you've done and have compassion for what you haven't done.

I was a fake fan of myself.
I would only offer my support when
I "beat everyone else" or when I "won."

But I'm in the music business, not sports. There's no even playing field where we all compete and there's no scoreboard . . . no finite "ending" so there's really no winners or losers. Just egos clashing and people battling themselves for the whole world to watch.

You are a fair-weather fan of yourself if you only celebrate when you win.

Real fans have cheered through thirty losing seasons in a row. Diehard fans of losing franchises should be studied. If you ask a diehard fan of a consistently losing franchise where their adoration comes from, they champion the small wins.

"We improved our hitting," they say proudly.

They celebrate drafting a great rookie. They are experts in seeing the silver lining.

"

Be a diehard fan of yourself.

"

"

People naturally want to receive you when you receive yourself.

"

I'm getting better at having moments of gratitude. I tend to only take the time to reflect and self-recognize when I have done something grandiose. Maybe that's something I need to start implementing into my day-to-day—waking up and doing a gratitude journal.

My unwillingness to self-recognize is arrogance; it came from a belief that I shouldn't need to celebrate myself.

"

Self-recognition is a skill.

"

It's something you have to practice. If you've never done it before, it might feel awkward. You might think, *I shouldn't need to clap for myself*. But you do.

I'd been chasing approval and validation from everyone else and love from everyone else and forgiveness from everyone else and patience from everyone else. It turns out that what I'd been chasing was me. I did need all those things, but I needed them from myself.

Be the fan that you need in your life. You need someone who supports you through the highs and lows, and doesn't burn your jersey if you have a bad game. Cheer for yourself along the way, hold yourself accountable, and recognize and celebrate the small wins so that when you get the trophy, you don't check to see whose name is on it.

CHAPTER

07

STILL

YOU'RE OKAY, YOU GOT YOU

In my twenties I often felt like I was in survival mode. I felt unsafe and unprotected the majority of the time. My nervous system was out of whack, and I was constantly having to calm myself down. That's why I was drinking a lot. That's why I was promiscuous. And that's why I was overeating. All these things were acts of self-soothing and self-regulating. That's also why I was always in the studio, because music was the only way I was able to make sense of everything else going on in my life. Down in my studio I could get it all out, even if I didn't quite understand it. Music is really your soul trying to communicate. I would get a release from making music. Working on songs quieted the chatter in my head—the overthinking that can spiral through my head and hijack my brain. I would sit in the studio every day for hours because it distracted me from my anxiety.

Outside of the studio I struggled to quiet the

chatter. I had a big meeting in Los Angeles and afterward my overthinking took over. Beforehand I pressured myself, *Oh, my God, this meeting has to go so fucking well.* Afterward I second-guessed myself—questioning why I said certain things, wondering why I didn't say other things. Worrying about whether I'd messed the whole thing up. Was everything going to be okay?

All of my overthinking stems from one one question: Am I going to be okay? When that energy sparks up, it's my responsibility to assure myself. That's what I needed as a kid, but now it's my job to father my inner child. When I do that, the overwhelming fear and anxiety recedes.

You're going to be okay. It's all good. I got you.

A constant source of my worry was my mother. My whole life, I've felt like my mother's been standing on the edge of a ledge and I've been afraid that I would say something that would make her jump. Everything felt like life or death. That's an insane place to be as a kid. As I got older, this fear didn't go away. I never felt okay and I never trusted that my family would be okay.

That played out especially intensely in my relationship with my mom. If she said something alarming and then didn't text me back for hours, I would start calling my brother and sister asking if they had talked to Mom. If she and I had an argument, my usual instinct would be to drive over to her house, swoop in, and "save" her. I wanted to know that she was okay.

Recently, she sent my brother, sister, and me this long text telling us that she was going off the grid. Usually I'd interpret that as a cry for help and would rush over. But this time I took a beat: I talked to Connor.

"Look," he told me, "she said she wants to go off the grid, and she wants to be left alone. Leave her alone."

For once, I didn't run over. Although I did spend the next three days talking to my dad, Frank, and my sister, Gianna. Everyone said, "She's fine. She'll be okay." I wasn't sure, but I sat tight. Then she popped back up.

"Hey, can I come to your show this weekend?" she asked casually. And a few hours later she was over at my house swimming.

That was a wake-up call. She had figured it out. I'd been freaking the fuck out for thirty years about her, when she's fine. She spirals easily but that's work that she has to do. It's got nothing to do with me. She would be okay. My whole family would be okay. It's not my responsibility to save them.

"

I CAN'T SAVE MY MOM FROM THE HOLE SHE DIGS BY GOING DOWN INTO THE HOLE WITH HER.

"

And yet, that's what I would do all the time. I'd be completely emotionally entangled and right there with her, as opposed to empowering her to pull herself out of the hole.

When someone is flapping their arms and screaming out that they are drowning, but you can see that their feet are firmly, safely, on the ground, you do not need to jump in and save them. They're not drowning; they are panicking. What they need is not to be saved, but to be reminded that they can feel their feet on the ground, that they can save themselves.

My emotional life was constantly enmeshed with and affected by the emotional lives of the people I cared about most. This isn't healthy. It's called emotional entanglement. When my girl was distraught about something that didn't have anything to do with me, I would get pulled into her emotional forcefield. If someone I loved and was emotionally connected to was having a bad day, then I would have a bad day. That felt like caring; that felt like love. But it's not. It's fucked up. It is possible and it is okay for her to have a bad day and for me to have a good day.

If someone you care deeply about spirals unhealthily, you do not have to enter their spiral; you do not have to react to their situation. Instead, you can offer your support by saying something like, "That sounds really tough. Is there anything I can do to help?"

Connor introduced me to the concept of individuation, which is our own maturation process. It is basically being able to separate your identity and emotions from the people you love. I needed to be able to see clearly: This is who Mom is. This is who Dad is. This is who I am and who I want to become. Understanding those distinctions is important to becoming emotionally sovereign.

Emotional sovereignty is being responsible for your own emotions and your emotions alone. Being emotionally sovereign is empowering and contagious. It not only allows you to have discernment with how you respond to your emotions, but lets you realize that autonomy is inspiring to those around you. By not entangling them in your emotions, you are modeling that they too are capable of taking sole responsibility for their emotions. This doesn't mean that you can't have a support system. You can and should. But, being emotionally sovereign allows you the freedom to move through the world directing your energy in the most productive way, rather than dumping energy into blackholes of fear and insecurity.

Whenever my mom spiraled I reacted. I'd get very frantic and start worrying: *Are you okay? Are we going to be okay? Is everything okay?* All this excited energy would surge up in me and I'd want to do something. Most often, my impulse was to run and try to fix her situation. But what I most needed to do was to be still.

"

STILLNESS IS THE ANTIDOTE TO BEING REACTIVE.

"

Understanding what is yours to hold, and knowing where your emotions start and stop, allows you to have stillness.

Stillness can only be achieved once you know you're going to be okay. Tell your inner child they are going to be okay. Assure yourself that the people you care about are going to be okay. You're just having a bad day. Your mom's just having a bad day, but they're going to be okay. So sit still. Have a quiet mind. Hold yourself. You will be okay.

"

THEY'RE NOT DROWNING, THEY'RE
PANICKING. YOU DON'T NEED TO
JUMP INTO THEIR PANIC SPIRAL.
THEY JUST NEED TO BE REMINDED
THAT THEIR FEET ARE ON THE
GROUND AND THAT THEY CAN
SAVE THEMSELVES.

"

In the past, I had so many emotions, but I didn't know what they all were. I was either letting them spill out or keeping them bottled up. The result was chaos. I spent much of my twenties emotionally entangled, not emotionally sovereign. My emotions were constantly merging with the emotions of the people around me.

You can learn how to discipline yourself and have control over your emotions. When you can control your emotions, you feel less of a need to control everything around you. I tried to control everything because I never trusted that things would be okay, that my mother would be okay, or that I would. That lack of trust ended up manifesting in so many other aspects of my life—with my manager, with my girl, with my fans. My impulse is to micromanage and emotionally monitor, to be super hypervigilant to make sure everything goes according to plan. When you understand your emotions, you can make space between your feelings and your actions.

Even if you are not a natural writer, writing can be a very powerful process that helps you identify what you're feeling and where those feelings are coming from. There's something about putting pen on paper (not in Notes on your phone!) and writing down a bunch of shit that you're keeping bottled up. After I write, I feel like the bottle is not quite as full anymore. A lot of us walk around with our bottle filled to the brim with our pain, insecurities, and trauma. We get reactive to any slight inconvenience in our day-to-day life. A small thing can tip our bottle so that all the stuff we've been holding spills out. But if you write, the act can empty that bottle just enough so that an inconvenience might tilt it, but the bottle won't be full enough to spill out all your trauma on the people around you.

Therapy helps too. That's a place where you can not only empty the bottle, but examine what's inside and where it is coming from.

In therapy I learned that a lot of my anxiety, my perfectionism, and my overthinking stems from the fears of my inner child. I was always worrying about whether everything would be okay. Now, as an adult, it's my job to father myself, to father that little boy.

"

STRIVE TO BE SOMEONE WHO IS CAPABLE—PHYSICALLY, MENTALLY, AND EMOTIONALLY.

"

You feel the full range of emotion, the rage and sadness and joy, but you have control over the feelings and you know how to navigate them. Clarity about what you're feeling helps you take a beat and communicate clearly about what you're feeling and why. (At least on the good days.) In order to do this, embrace your insecurities rather than resist them. Acknowledge the needs of your inner child; address them.

You're gonna be okay.

08

MONEY ON ME

THE POWER OF CHOICE

"

Every day you wake up
      and have a choice.

"

Every day you wake up and have a choice. Having confidence in your decision-making skills is ultimately a by-product of self-trust. One way to develop self-trust is to bet on yourself.

When you start making healthier decisions about where to put your energy and your emotions, you feel so much better about who you are as a person. You are in control of your decisions, your choices, and your energy.

So many of us are not even aware we're holding the power of choice. You can turn your life around. You can eat better. You can treat yourself better. Exercising control over your decisions gives you a lot more confidence.

In the music industry it's very common to outsource the creative. You can hire a producer and hire a writer, and they can hand you a hit song. What happens when the song becomes a hit though? Next time you go to the studio you're going to assume you need to call them again in order to reenact the success.

A big reason why, especially early on, I wanted to handle all the aspects of making a song myself was because I wanted to know what I was capable of. How big can a song be if I'm the only one who worked on it? After all, a song is just hundreds of decisions compiled into one audio experience.

What tempo should the song be?

What kind of hi hats do I want?

What kind of snares?

What kind of kick drum?

What rhythm should they all be doing?

What lyrics work with this?

What words sound good over this beat?

Should I add harmonies?

How much reverb should I put on the chorus?

Should I echo this part?

Should I drop the beat out at this part and bring it back here?

Each song is a thousand decisions that I feel confident about.

When my songs go platinum or achieve outlier-level success, I never look at them like, *Wow this song went platinum.* I recognize that every decision I made went platinum.

Of course, I've made decisions that haven't yielded extreme levels of success, but what matters is that I know that I'm capable of extreme success.

The success I feel in the studio has trickled into the rest of my life. I'm able to make decisions quickly and confidently because I trust myself, I trust my gut, I trust that I'm going to make the right decisions. I have confidence in my decision-making skills regardless of what the endeavor is because through music I developed self-trust.

You have to bet on yourself enough times early

on so that you can see yourself win and lose. You need to have experience with both outcomes. It's important because some people think, "I need to take every shot. That's what betting on myself means." No, it doesn't mean take every shot. It means trust yourself to know that you're going to make the right decision in the moment. That might mean pass. That might mean shoot. What's important is that you trust yourself either way.

Trust yourself to start making small decisions in your life and accept the fact that you're not always going to get it right. That's part of the experience. Some decisions won't be the best decisions, but compounded over time, if you are constantly making the decisions in your life, (instead of letting parents, partners, or bosses decide for you) over time, the self-trust builds and so does the confidence.

I stand by my decisions—they usually turn out well, one way or another. What gets me into trouble is a lack of decision-making, instances when I wasn't even aware that I was making a choice. Moments when I was just coasting along thoughtlessly, neither here nor there, just going through the motions in an unintentional, undisciplined life.

How can you bet on yourself when you're not aware that you're holding the chips.

In my twenties, I was very disciplined and intentional about my music, but outside of the studio I was coasting along, largely unaware. That's the way I had been living for a while. Part of the breakdown I had before canceling the tour was that I had finally recognized that I had a choice, that I could make the decision to turn it around. I could decide to put my money on me.

> "
> **You are holding the chips.**
> **You can bet on yourself.**
> "

Be awake. Be conscious. Wake up to the idea that the power of choice is real, and you can make a decision right now to be exactly who you want to be.

I'd started working on *Santiago* in the summer of 2021. I basically had the whole album together before I canceled my tour a year later. But after I started therapy, I thought my verses sounded fluffy and vapid. Not the honest grappling with big questions that had inspired me when I reread *The Alchemist*. I decided that my only choice was to scrap the whole album.

I was dejected. I'd let myself down. I'd had a lot of people work on the project with me, and I would have to let all of them down too. I'd made the whole album, but I still couldn't name what my treasure was. What was I really chasing? I thought about the months I'd spent in therapy working on disciplining myself, being emotionally sovereign, and acknowledging myself.

In short, I'd been working on me.

I was the treasure.

Treasure is self-mastery.

None of us will ever be able to completely master ourselves. But what a thing to go after, because you can always see progress in it. You always have the choice to get better at being the son or brother or partner; you can treat your body better, better control your emotions, and constantly hone your gifts so that you are bringing your best to the world.

Maybe I didn't need to scrap *Santiago*. The skeleton was good. Maybe I needed to rewrite all my verses. I needed to put everything I was learning into the music. I believed in the music. I believed in the message. I believed in the people I brought on to help me with the album. I believed in my decisions, so I made the choice to continue to bet on myself and finish what I had started.

09

FREED UP

FREE YOURSELF FROM YOUR INNER CRITIC

Our brains are designed to resist change because change is unfamiliar, which could mean danger. However, the unknown is where the potential for growth lives. We must hop the fence of our fear in order to flourish and become a better version of ourselves.

I was chained to my inner critic. I thought that if I stopped beating myself up and instead offered compassion, I would get complacent and lose my drive. That's only because my drive was being fueled by darkness instead of light. It was my need to be liked, approved, and recognized that was pushing me to achieve. In one of our sessions, Connor introduced me to a profound concept: Light motivation versus dark motivation. Those are dark motivations because they're based in fear. Fear of not being liked, approved, and recognized. Instead, I replaced them with the passion for my craft, the enjoyment of seeing progress, my desire to contribute something positive to people, and my genuine adoration for connection. Those are light motivations because they are based in love.

I had experienced an ass beating from myself and the world for mistakes I had made. There was a new fear that developed from this. I was afraid of more success. More success meant less room for error. It amplified the need for perfection, which caused extreme anxiety. I was at odds internally. Part of me wanted to see myself progress and achieve more. Part of me didn't want to get a hit again.

"

FEAR HAD WON THE WAR AGAINST MY AMBITION & MY GREATNESS WAS A POW.

"

Our greatness is often restrained by our fear. We don't allow ourselves to achieve and be "great" out of fear of criticism and judgment. My inner critic was brutal. I was my own bully. Until I freed myself from my own judgment and criticism, I was always going to be shackled to other people's judgment and criticisms.

Reconciling with the "mob" is never going to work. I needed to reconcile with myself. Mistakes are inevitable. I'm allowed to make mistakes. That is just part of the human experience.

I spent my twenties seeking validation. I wanted people to tell me that I was right. I wanted that approval.

People are so quick to react to things on social media because they want their perspective to be validated. I spent years falling into that trap. I was always hunting for things to react to in the culture that I wanted to be a part of.

I kept trying to find things where it was like,

Why are y'all clapping for that?
That's fucked up. Look at me.

I was asking other people to give me something that I hadn't given myself. I needed to approve and validate myself.

I try to treat social media differently now. I don't feel the need to insert myself unprovoked into a discourse.

I'm my own board of approval. When something triggers an emotional reaction, we stop and ask ourselves: *What part of me is being triggered and why? Where is that coming from? What is it that we really want to say? And could I just put this in a song?* Usually, by the end of the meeting the board had decided not to comment.

If I had been driven by light and not dark

motivations, there'd have been a lot less stomping of my feet and yelling at the industry to notice me, and a lot more celebration of making music and chasing mastery in the field. Anytime I accomplished something extraordinary, I could have clapped for myself instead of screaming, *SEE, LOOK!* I blocked myself from feeling the victories because I was too focused on showing everyone I won.

You can be extremely successful off dark motivations. But that is not sustainable. When I started working out, I hated it because my desire for fitness came from a place of shame. My inner critic said, *Well, too bad. You're too heavy. You're fucking disgusting. You need to work out.* I lost the weight, but I did not gain my support.

Losing weight and getting in shape wasn't a labor of love. It was an exercise in shame. I still felt bad about myself, and I knew it wasn't because of my outward appearance. When you achieve the external results but still don't feel good internally, that should alert you that a shift is required.

My whole attitude toward exercise has changed. Going to the gym used to be a punishment; now its a celebration. That's light motivation.

If the only reason you want to achieve is to get approval and validation and recognition from other people, then if you receive recognition, will you lose your motivation? That is a scary prospect. But if you honor the gift, if you put in the effort, if you want to see progress and continuously work toward mastery in something you love, if you chase after excellence, that's something that, regardless of external recognition, will inspire you to keep going. Dark motivation has an expiration date. Light motivation stays fresh forever.

10

WAVES

KEEP FLOATING AND MAINTAIN PERSPECTIVE

Life is a series of waves.

Sometimes you're riding on top of the waves, everything is smooth. Sometimes you're getting pummeled by them. Sometimes you're just floating, wondering if the "action" is behind you and all that's left to do is to float until you die.

When I was first trying to blow up as a musician, I was in the floating stage. I had hopes that my wave was going to come, but I had to rely on faith. When a wave of success finally came, and I blew up in 2016, I thought that I was going to be riding on top of it forever.

By the end of 2017 that wave had crashed. My parents' marriage finally reached a breaking point. I got my first taste of mass internet hate and media scrutiny, which inevitably led to fugitive fans. I was devastated and thought another wave would never come. That is where perspective comes in.

Floating after experiencing both the beauty and the madness of the waves can leave you with conflicting feelings. On the one hand, you desperately want to ride another wave; on the other, you don't want it to crash. But waves crash; it is in their nature. All you can do is keep floating.

The floating time is a real test of patience. Patience is faith—in yourself and in the fact that another wave will come. Don't sit in the in-between time and rob yourself of the present.

When I'm on top of a career wave, I'm doing a show in one place, a promo in another. It feels like all those late-night studio sessions paid off. The excitement around me and my music is palpable. The fans are more activated than ever. It's fun but my schedule is crazy, and I don't have as much time for family or for my home life. I don't have time to replenish. But once a wave has crested I am at the house more. I have more bandwidth for my family, my friends, myself. That time is nourishing. Both the top of the wave and the floating period have value.

You don't need to spend every day thinking about when the next wave is going to come—you know it's coming, because that's what waves do. Be with your family. Read a book. Better yourself. Feed yourself. And acknowledge where you have been so far.

The floating time is also a learning period; use it to reflect and reassess. Reflect on your success. Acknowledge how great it was. How did you catch that wave? What made it crash? Learn from the process. What can you take with you when the next wave lifts you up?

There's no avoiding the waves unless you get out of the ocean . . . but then good luck avoiding yourself as you have to watch the waves from the shore and wonder about the what-if: What if you were able to manage the highs and lows?

When you accept the nature of waves, that they are both constant and impermanent, it is easier to have a deeper sense of gratitude, perspective, peace, and foresight.

By now, I've had enough peaks and valleys to know that everything comes in waves and that every wave will be different.

"

DON'T COMPARE THE WAVES. ACCEPT THEM AS THEY COME. ENJOY THEM WHILE THEY LAST.

"

Now when things are going great I celebrate instead of worrying about when the wave is going to crash. Inevitably, the wave *is* going to crash, so enjoy the ride, have gratitude for it. And when you're back to floating, don't sit there and freak the fuck out thinking, *Oh my god, a wave is never going to come again.* That's what waves do. That's just the nature of waves, and that's the nature of life. Good things come and then they pass. So do bad things. The question is: What will you do in between?

I wish I had known this earlier on in my career because it would have given me the ability to not get so frantic and paranoid. It might have stopped me from switching into survival mode. When I'm high on a wave, I sometimes still catch myself starting to worry about when it is going to end. But by now, I've seen how it goes. When I catch a big song, I know the wave is going to crash. But

I remember the nature of waves and then I allow myself to enjoy the ride.

When you are having a big moment, enjoy it.
Stay present.
Post about it.
Tell your friends.
Celebrate the wave.

It's such a better energy to enjoy riding on the wave than worrying about when it's going to crash and how long you will be floating until the next wave comes, or worrying whether a wave is ever going to come again.

You're in the ocean.
The waves will come.

11

ENJOY THE VIEW

LOOK OUT THE WINDOW

BE FAST AND YOU JOIN THE
SCENERY . . . SLOW DOWN AND
YOU ENJOY THE SCENERY

— "ENJOY THE VIEW"

Life is a train; you are the engineer. Imagine that you're driving and the speed at which the train moves is determined by how present you are. The train moves fast and the scenery outside is a blur when you're always thinking about "the next thing." On the other hand, when you're present, the train slows down and you look out the window and suddenly the scenery isn't a blur anymore. It's vivid, vibrant, alive.

But most of us, most of the time, not only think that we're on a bullet train, but we don't even think we're driving it. Just passengers watching life fly by.

Life moves at whatever speed you move it at. Look out the window every once in a while. Enjoy the view.

Don't be so busy making a living that you forget to make a life. I always loved that saying, but I never knew the value of it until I got burnt out due to my lack of balance. Metaphorically speaking, I was always so focused on getting to the next city that I couldn't even tell you what the weather was in the city that I was currently in. That's basically how my twenties went. Go go go. Chasing after what, though? Success, self-love, both? Death? Maybe—sure as hell was running fast enough.

Back when I'd begun making *Santiago*, I was burnt out. I numbed myself with the speed of the train I was driving. I numbed myself with what I put in my body. I numbed myself with work.

I was consumed with how fast the train was going. Imagine having to finish a lifetime amount of work in between train stops. Sitting on the train and hearing the conductor say,

"Next stop _____."

It was always my stop that was next. I was always in a scramble to finish EVERYTHING I ever wanted to do in life in the next ten minutes or else. I brought all that pressure into the studio. So, I drank till I couldn't hear the conductor.

My music was supposed to be the cure-all medicine. It had to get me respect, love, money, happiness, and worth. I needed it to give me everything. But that's not fair to the music, that's not fair to the art, and that's not fair to the creative side of me. I think of it like a relay race, with each leg represented by the different aspects of me— Fitness Russ, Emotional Russ, Mental Russ, Family Russ. All of those other Russes wouldn't show up for the race, then I'd pass the baton off to Creative Russ and say, *"Go make all of us back here feel perfect, because we're all fucked up and we're all counting on you and we're not doing shit about it, by the way, because we don't know what to do.*

You've got to do it for us. You've got to save all of us." That's too much pressure on one guy. That's too much pressure on the music.

All the work I've done has taught me to slow down the train. To look out the window. To enjoy the view. Now I try to feed all the different parts of me. I go to the gym, and Fitness Russ feels good about himself. I read, and Mental Russ feels good about himself. I do therapy, and Emotional Russ feels good about himself. I spend time with my niece and loved ones, and Family Russ feels good about himself. The result is that there's a lot less pressure on Creative Russ.

Making progress in all these other areas of my life has meant the stakes in the studio aren't as high because the music isn't having to give me everything anymore. The Musician Russ gets to go into the studio and enjoy it.

Now getting back into the studio and making

music is fun. It's not confined by anything—not an album concept, not the need to go platinum or number one. I'm making music for music's sake. I'm enjoying the view.

What's the point of the labor if you never taste the fruit?

Work hard in whatever field you choose and strive to be the greatest version of yourself you can be. And create a balanced life. I'm an artist and life fuels my art. Too little life and my art suffers. Too much art and my life suffers. I think that's true for all of us. Too little life and our work suffers. Too much life and our work suffers. The 24/7 grind-mode community is toxic. Humans need balance. We need moments with nature, moments with people we love doing regular shit, moments to do something that satisfies our inner child. All these things fill us up. Without them our well is dry, and you can send the bucket down as many times as you want, but if you don't fill yourself up, the bucket will come back empty every time.

Your best work comes when you have a healthy work-life balance. This is especially evident in creative work. My biggest hit songs did not come from me being a studio rat, sitting down here, six days in a row, looking at the walls. All my best songs and all my biggest songs have always emerged from regular life. They come from the balance. They come from looking at the scenery. They come from driving around with a girl after work or enjoying a meal with family. Life nourishes and inspires us.

The harsh reality is that the only final destination is death. Why are you rushing to get there?

"

THE JOURNEY IS THE TREASURE.
WHEN YOU ENJOY THE VIEW,
YOU ARRIVE.

"

12

I LOVE ME

DO NOT TRADE AUTHENTICITY FOR ACCEPTANCE

Being myself felt unsafe from an early age.

My dad switched jobs often while I was growing up, so we moved around a lot. Each time we picked up our life, I felt alone and isolated, uprooted from the world I knew and from my friends. We moved when I was a baby, when I was five, again when I was six, but the toughest move was when we came to Atlanta just as I was starting eighth grade.

I showed up to school on the first day of eighth grade wearing what I was comfortable in—AND1 jersey and shorts, black and red Air Force 1s, and an earring.

A kid I knew told me that people were calling me a wigger behind my back. I had no idea what that was. But I did know that no one that looked like me, dressed like me.

I was twelve. I was the new kid. All I wanted was to fit in and make friends. Instead, I was ridiculed. Fear bloomed in me like a black hole.

I hadn't been accepted. I wasn't good enough. I choked on my panic. I wanted to survive socially, but in my adolescent brain that meant I couldn't be who I was; I had to change.

When I got home that afternoon, I begged my mom and dad to buy me new shorts and collared shirts. I wanted what everyone else was wearing. By the next day I had taken the earring out and swapped the basketball gear for Bermuda shorts and a polo shirt.

Overnight I had learned to self-reject and self-deprecate. I had been so embarrassed by who I was because it wasn't "good enough" for the environment I was in. I gave up who I was in order to be accepted. I didn't realize the impact and the effect that would have, the trauma that that caused, and the way it would carry over into my adult life.

Being a white guy in the rap game felt like being twelve all over again. I was the new kid and I didn't fit in and I desperately wanted to. There were times when I was doing stuff just because everyone else was, and I thought, *Well, if I do that maybe they'll like me too*. Whether that was blowing $50k at a strip club, sleeping with a bunch of random women, associating with people I shouldn't have been, getting into fights, etc., I didn't care. I was in.

When it comes to the industry, I didn't know how to play the game authentically to myself. I wasn't living an authentic experience because of my porous boundaries. When we don't have boundaries, we end up acting out of alignment with who we are. Sometimes that means acting like someone we're not in an attempt to get people to like us. That is what happens when your insecurities are behind the wheel.

We often trade authenticity for social acceptance. The less you like yourself the more important other people liking you is. You do not need to give up yourself to be accepted. You simply need to accept yourself.

When you distance yourself from the authentic version of who you are, it is harder for you to know how to be authentic. When your insecurities are driving and you're in the passenger seat, you're going to be weaving all over the road, heading toward things that don't align with who you are authentically—whether that's wearing shit you don't actually want to wear, talking in a way that isn't true to you, or behaving in ways that don't reflect who you really are.

"

INSECURITIES FLARE UP AND HIJACK YOUR IDENTITY, BUT YOU DON'T HAVE TO SURRENDER.

"

You can slide into the driver's seat and take control of the wheel so that your actions are in alignment with your authentic self.

When I liked myself less and my insecurities were at the wheel, I was a lot more reactive, and I was always looking for external validation and acceptance to quell them. It was kind of like my twelve-year-old self was screaming, *ACCEPT ME!* to the entire eighth grade.

Like everyone, I'm a work in progress. Recently, there was an article that said something about the illusion of the "Russ Method" and posited that I'd been leading artists down a destructive path with my philosophy of self-sufficiency. They even went so far as to accuse me of not actually making the music myself. In the past, my insecurities would have taken over. I would have reacted publicly because I would have seen it as a threat to my acceptance and a threat to the perception of my story externally. But this time, I didn't say anything. I read it and I asked myself, *Is it true?*

Sometimes that's all you need to do with a negative comment or a comment that bothers you. If it's not true, you can simply decide not to respond to it.

I knew the piece was bogus. I ran it by my board—and all the versions of me agreed. I didn't need to address the untruth, because I didn't need the external validation. I knew the truth about myself and I had accepted it.

At some point your insecurities will take over, but when that happens, at least, you will have awareness. The more you practice and reflect, the clearer your sense of self will be.

You have to decide if your everyday choices align with your authentic self. You also have to get really clear about who your authentic self is. Are you happy with how you show up in the world? Are you happy with how you handle things? Are you happy with how you are? Because there is an alternative path that you can walk, but it's scary.

"

EVERY DAY YOU HAVE A CHOICE OF WHO YOU WANT TO BE.

"

Do you want to be the kind of person who gets up with ten minutes of sunlight? Do you want to be the person who gets up and goes to the gym, spends time with the people you love, and is able to create meaning? Do you want to put on a costume and pretend to be someone else? Who do you want to be?

Be aware that you do have a choice. Be aware of whether you've been choosing the wrong path, be aware that that path no longer aligns with who you want to be. You need to be disciplined and make a conscious effort to choose a path that aligns with who you want to be.

Imagine your future self coming up to you. What do they look like? How do they speak? How do they think? What kind of life do they have? Are the choices you're making in your present life congruent with the identity of your future self?

Looking at your choices through the lens of identity can put things into perspective.

When I started getting healthier, I made a choice to start drinking less. I didn't want my identity to be: heavy drinker. That doesn't mean that I can't ever drink; it's just that from an identity standpoint, I'm not a heavy drinker. I occasionally drink versus I am a heavy drinker.

You can apply that to anything you do or think. This is not about being judgmental; it is about finding motivation from your future self to start making choices on a day-to-day basis that are in harmony with that version.

The identity that I'm trying to create is someone who tries to choose the healthy path across the board—mentally, physically, creatively. I want to be somebody who's on their shit. In my twenties the rockstar lifestyle was attractive. That was a fun identity, and it was fine for as long as it was fine, but I reached a point where that version of myself had carried me as far as he could. It was time for the next version.

Each version of yourself should carry you closer to your authentic self.

As you keep evolving, moving closer and closer to the treasure, you keep choosing yourself. Each time you do, you're stating, simply and clearly:

I love me.

"

**SELF-LOVE IS ABOUT HONORING
WHO YOU ARE AND MORE
IMPORTANTLY WHO YOU'RE NOT.**

"

13

TUNNEL VISION

PROGRESS IS THE
ULTIMATE PURSUIT

THE JOURNEY'S THE TREASURE IF I AIN'T MOVIN', I'M LOSIN', FOR REAL

— "TUNNEL VISION"

A lot of people feel lost because they don't know where they're going, and when you don't know where you're going, you end up everywhere and nowhere.

Know where you are headed.

Know what your treasure is.

I used to think that my ultimate pursuit was a platinum album, being on an esoteric list of greatest rappers ever, or having the most awards. All of that is vapid. It's also external and not in my control. I can make what I think is the best music in the world, but if people don't listen to it, it won't go platinum. If people don't give me awards, then I won't get any. If the world doesn't say that I'm the greatest rapper ever, then I'm not (according to them).

"

PROGRESS IS THE ULTIMATE PURSUIT. IT IS A TROPHY THAT EVERYONE CAN WIN.

"

Spoiler alert: You will never reach complete self-mastery. But you can always make progress, and it will be so fulfilling at every checkpoint.

In my twenties, I had tunnel vision on my career. But while my career thrived, my physical and mental health declined. My relationships declined. If I'd had tunnel vision on my relationships, then my career would decline. I'm very black-and-white sometimes, and I didn't know that the answer was somewhere in the middle.

Having tunnel vision on progress means making all of you great—it means improving your physical and mental health, developing your career, your craft, your purpose, and having balance. It means all of those things because the treasure is you, and you are not one thing.

If you have tunnel vision on progress, you're

going to become a better friend, a better partner, a better son, a better artist, a better everything.

ACROSS THE BOARD, I WANNA SEE WHAT MY BEST IS

— "Tunnel Vision"

When I made *Santiago*, I laid a lot on the line. I took a lot of risks—artistically, personally, and financially—and I didn't want to get fixated on the commercial outcome, because this project was about the opposite of external approval. I knew I shouldn't need validation from external sources, like the Grammys, but I was wrestling with how to remain ambitious without wanting validation from Billboard or the Grammys.

The secret is decreasing the value from any external validation. When *Santiago* was about to come out, I had to interrogate why I still wanted a number one album and a Grammy.

I shifted my intention—the *Why?* if you will. I want a Grammy and a number one album because I've never had either. They mark progress.

"

USE PROGRESS AS YOUR BENCHMARK FOR SUCCESS.

"

Wanting progress is healthy. Wanting it can be motivating and rewarding. It gets toxic when you make markers of progress your enemy. Wanting to achieve isn't wrong. It's the intention behind it. If the intention is progress, that's pure, that's a light motivation.

I am still getting better at recognizing progress. Sometimes that requires zooming in to acknowledge progress on the most granular level. Seeing all the small wins can help you keep perspective when things don't go how you wanted them to.

When I put out *Santiago*, I was so proud of the music and the rollout. I had made exactly what I wanted and put it out exactly how I wanted. But Billboard and Luminate, the companies in collaboration that verify the numbers, took away ten thousand of my sales on the grounds that I'm not allowed to incentivize fans to buy albums. Meanwhile, they allow other artists to fake their streams and do merch bundles (pretty incentivizing, if you ask me). I was so angry. There's a lot of competition around releases. When an album is released, the first week of sales is a big talking point in the industry and a major measure of success.

When I explained the situation to my therapist and said, "This is ruining my whole moment of celebration. They're taking my progress away."

Connor was quick to check me. "No," he said while looking right at me through our screens. "They're taking the external perception of your progress away. But your own knowing of your progress can't be taken away."

Damn. I'd been chasing validation again. I knew I'd made progress, but Billboard and Luminate made it seem to the world that I hadn't. I had to accept that I can't reconcile with the world. I had to reconcile with myself. It was me who needed to acknowledge the progress that I'd made. That wasn't anyone else's job. I had to reaffirm what I believed: that it was me all along.

Learning to separate the external from the internal is really tough for me. I had to understand that Billboard might have taken away my external perception of progress, but not my internal knowing of my progress. It was a cosmic fucking joke. Afterall, *Santiago* was about leaning into internal validation and not getting caught up in the external perception of my progress. This was the universe giving me a field test.

I had to acknowledge that I did everything I could. I had to remind myself of all the pieces I had made progress on—the rollout, the money spent, and the actual music itself. I had made progress on all those fronts. I had done more than I'd ever done. I had to acknowledge all the work I put in so that I could celebrate myself.

I also needed to recognize that *Santiago* was the most vulnerable and intimate album that I'd ever made—and my fans had shown up for it—acknowledging my pain, acknowledging my insecurities, inviting my fans in on a deep level that allowed me to be more authentic with them in my music, and allowed me to make something like *Santiago*. The smoke and mirrors were gone. I feel fucked up, just like you. By making an album about what I was going through, I broke down a wall between me and my fans, and they came with me on my journey.

Did I reach my commercial ambitions?

No.

But did I achieve progress?

I did.

14

ADVENTURE

FAITH IS A CATALYST FOR WONDER

THINK ABOUT HOW FAR YOU'VE
COME JUST REMEMBER
YOU'RE NOT LOST YOU'RE ON AN
ADVENTURE

— "ADVENTURE"

Life is an adventure full of inevitable surprise and change. We humans tend to not like change because change means new. New means unknown. Unknown means out of our control. Scary.

I have spent a lot of my energy fixating on outcomes leaving little to no room to see what the universe has in store. When you send the universe your wishlist and have the mindset of "nothing more, nothing less," you block the possibility of receiving a gift that you didn't even know you wanted. Like waking up and unexpectedly seeing a video that Rihanna had posted of her wearing a bikini and walking in slow motion with my song "Best On Earth" playing—that was a wondrous gift from the universe. Part of why my accomplishments didn't always register with me was because I was expecting them. There was no element of wonder because I was fixated on the outcome instead of having faith in the adventure.

Lack of faith is an insecurity. It is a false sense of omnipotence—thinking you know better than a higher power. Control happens when there is no faith. If you're like me, you've probably tried controlling a lot of aspects of your life, if not every aspect. That stems from fear and lack of faith. That manifested in micromanaging my manager, yelling at coworkers, and getting no sleep because I would lay awake worried that I didn't do everything I could to control the outcome. I had to learn to let go.

"

SOMETIMES ADVENTURE MEANS GETTING OUT OF THE WAY AND FINDING OUT WHAT WILL HAPPEN.

"

Relinquish the need to control and resist everything that doesn't look exactly how you saw it in your head. What if things can turn out better than you can imagine?

It's okay and healthy to have specific goals, but we can't allow them to consume us to the point that we are opposed to other favorable outcomes. Connor told me, "Belief clings; faith allows space for possibility."

We need to leave room for the universe's hand to be present.

Life is an adventure, and rarely do things go exactly how we plan. Accept that. Do your best to influence what you can in a productive way and let go of trying to control the rest. Real power isn't control; it is faith in yourself and your ability to discover, to learn, to grow.

"

WHAT YOU DON'T KNOW DOESN'T HAVE TO BE A SOURCE OF FEAR; IT CAN BE A SOURCE OF WONDER.

"

After *Santiago* was released, I opened for Ed Sheeran. At soundcheck, I walked out onto the biggest stage I'd ever played. Standing up there in the cavernous, empty stadium, I saw my name light up the jumbotron. RUSS in big letters, bright above eighty thousand seats. That's a crazy marker of external recognition. Only there was no internal recognition to match it. I looked up and my stomach tightened. My imposter syndrome had kicked in, and instead of celebrating, I thought, *Holy fuck. What the fuck is going on? I don't deserve to be here.*

I could feel the pit of insecurity inside me, but I recognized what it was, and after soundcheck I went back to my dressing room and reminded myself: *I'm supposed to be here. I have enough faith in the universe to know that this is happening because it's supposed to be happening. I'm supposed to be here, and I'm here because I am ready.*

All I had to do was show up and do my best and leave some room for the universe to take care of the rest. However it goes is however it is going to go.

I stepped onto the stage of a stadium packed with people and did my set knowing that I was exactly where I was meant to be.

However, that moment of awareness wasn't enough to quiet the perfectionist in me. As soon as I stepped off the stage I asked my tour manager, "Did it look like I stumbled onstage?" Instead of soaking up the moment, I beat myself up. I zeroed in on what was not perfect. I nitpicked and criticized my performance, and myself. *Oh, you fucked up the word right there. You weren't perfect.*

In the past that would have sent me into a spiral of criticism. But I noticed my insecurity and stepped back and told myself, *It was good. No one gives a fuck about a minor stumble. It was awesome.* For the second time that evening, I used everything

I had been learning to pull myself back from the edge. I let go of trying to be perfect. I let go of trying to control the night. The adventure is being open to what will come.

Ed took the stage and the fans went wild. A couple songs into his set, he shouted me out and then, to my surprise, called me back out to perform with him. The energy in the stadium was insane. I looked out and felt a jolt of electricity.

When I stepped off stage, I smiled to myself.

The night had turned out better than I could have imagined. It's amazing what happens when you let go and walk confidently into the wonder of the unknown.

15

THE WIND

THE ANSWER IS IN THE MIRROR

MY CONNECTION WITH MYSELF IS
MY STRONGEST ALLIANCE

— "The Wind"

The journey to self-discovery is endless. Strive for goals, cultivate your ambition, get the plaques, but keep in mind that the real goal, the real treasure, is you. What you're really looking for is not out there. It's in you.

I spent a long time searching for a treasure I couldn't find. I took the journey to the pyramids. I tasted everything out there, and nothing fulfilled me. I'd been chasing approval, forgiveness, patience, validation, and love from everyone else. Then I realized that I needed to give those things to myself.

This is not a battle of you versus you. It is an alliance. It is you for you. You are your destination. You are your dream. You are everything you need. You are what you're looking for.

On my journey I've realized that every external obstacle along the way has been a mirror for an internal wound that I have been ignoring. Those wounds are there to inform us. They are opportunities for growth. I went looking for medicine in all the wrong places. A bottle, a random woman, a plaque, or a million dollars are all Band-Aids. It wasn't until I came home empty-handed and looked into the mirror of my own medicine cabinet that I found the cure.

It was me all along.

**what if you're the one
you've been waiting for?**

It

was

you

all

along

ACKNOWLEDGMENTS

I would like to thank my mom and my dad for
being the absolute best parents they could be
with the resources they had.
I love you both forever.

ABOUT THE AUTHOR

a human being